MY FIRST BOOK ABOUT

MICHIGAN

by Carole Marsh

This activity book has material which correlates with Michigan's Social Studies Content Standards. At every opportunity, we have tried to relate information to the History and Social Science, English, Science, Math, Civics, Economics, and Computer Technology SSCS directives. For additional information, go to our websites: **www.michiganexperience.com** or **www.gallopade.com**.

Correlates with Michigan's SSCS Social Studies Content Standards™

GALLOPADE INTERNATIONAL

Reading · Research · Reinforcement · Reference

Gallopade is proud to be a member of these educational organizations and associations:

SHOPA MEMBER™ School, Home, & Office Products Association

NSSEA

ASCD

The Michigan Experience Series

The Michigan Experience Paperback Book!

My First Pocket Guide to Michigan!

The Big Michigan Reproducible Activity Book

The Michigan Coloring Book!

My First Book About Michigan!

Michigan "Jography!": A Fun Run Through Our State

Michigan Jeopardy: Answers and Questions About Our State

The Michigan Experience! Sticker Pack

The Michigan Experience! Poster/Map

Discover Michigan CD-ROM

Michigan "GEO" Bingo Game

Michigan "HISTO" Bingo Game

A Word... From the Author

Do you know when I think children should start learning about their very own state? When they're born! After all, even when you're a little baby, this is your state too! This is where you were born. Even if you move away, this will always be your "home state." And if you were not born here, but moved here—this is still your state as long as you live here.

We know people love their country. Most people are very patriotic. We fly the U.S. flag. We go to Fourth of July parades. But most people also love their state. Our state is like a mini-country to us. We care about its places and people and history and flowers and birds.

As a child, we learn about our little corner of the world. Our room. Our home. Our yard. Our street. Our neighborhood. Our town. Even our county.

But very soon, we realize that we are part of a group of neighbor towns that make up our great state! Our newspaper carries stories about our state. The TV news is about happenings in our state. Our state's sports teams are our favorites. We are proud of our state's main tourist attractions.

From a very young age, we are aware that we are a part of our state. This is where our parents pay taxes and vote and where we go to school. BUT, we usually do not get to study about our state until we are in school for a few years!

So, this book is an introduction to our great state. It's just for you right now. Why wait to learn about your very own state? It's an exciting place and reading about it now will give you a head start for that time when you "officially" study our state history! Enjoy,

Carole Marsh

Michigan

Let's Have Words!

Make as many words as you can from the letters in the words:

THE WOLVERINE STATE!

Michigan
The 26th State

Do you know when Michigan became a state? Michigan became the 26th state in 1837.

Color Michigan red. Color Lake Michigan, Lake Huron, Lake Erie, and Lake Superior blue. Color the rest of the United States shown here green.

Michigan State Flag

The Michigan state flag was adopted in 1911. The state seal is shown on a blue background. Below the seal is a white banner with the state motto in black letters, and above the seal is a red banner with the U.S. motto *e pluribus unum.*

Color the Michigan state flag.

Michigan State Bird

Most states have a state bird. It should remind us that we need to "fly high" to achieve our goals. The Michigan state bird is the robin. Robins make their nests out of mud, grass, and twigs. They lay greenish blue eggs. Robins like to eat insects, worms, and fruit. They are named after an English bird with a much redder breast.

Circle your state bird, then color all the birds.

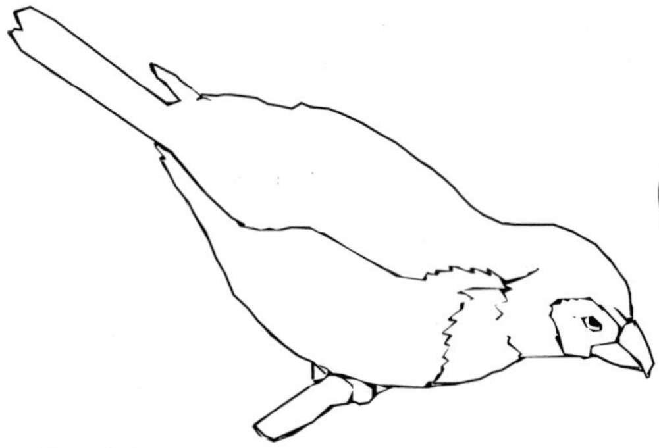

FINCH

GOOSE

ROBIN

BLUE JAY

EAGLE

DUCK

Michigan State Coat of Arms and Motto

The Michigan state Coat of Arms has a picture of a bald eagle in the center with a shield beneath it. On the left of the shield is an elk, and on the right is a moose. Across the top of the shield is the Latin word *tuebor*, which means "I will defend." Below the elk and moose is the state motto written in the Latin words, *Si quaeris peninsulam amoenam circumspice*, which translates "If you seek a pleasant peninsula, look around you." On a banner over the eagle is the phrase *e pluribus unum*, the motto of the United States, which means, "out of many, one." The shield is gold, and the banner above the eagle is red.

In 25 words or less, explain what the state motto means:

Color the state Coat of Arms.

Michigan State Flower

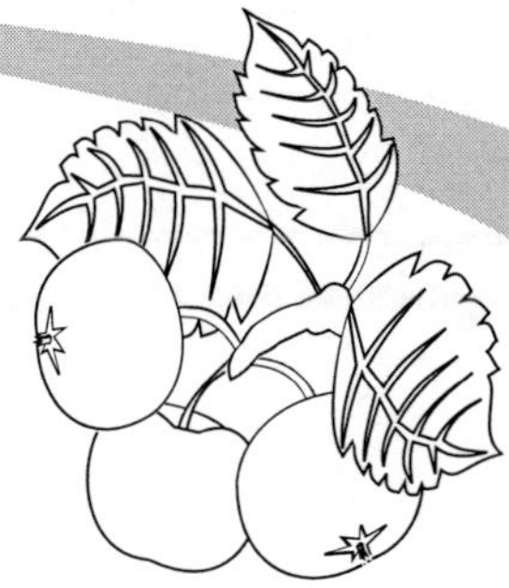

Every state has a favorite flower. The Michigan state flower is the apple blossom. It became the state flower in 1897. The apple blossom was chosen because Michigan is a leader in apple production.

Color the picture of our state flower.

Michigan
State Tree

Our state tree reminds us that our roots should run deep if we want to grow straight and tall! The state tree for Michigan is the white pine. It became the state tree in 1955. The white pine reminds us of the importance of our state's early lumber industry. White pines have soft, blue-green needles and are clustered in groups of five.

Finish drawing the white pine, then color it.

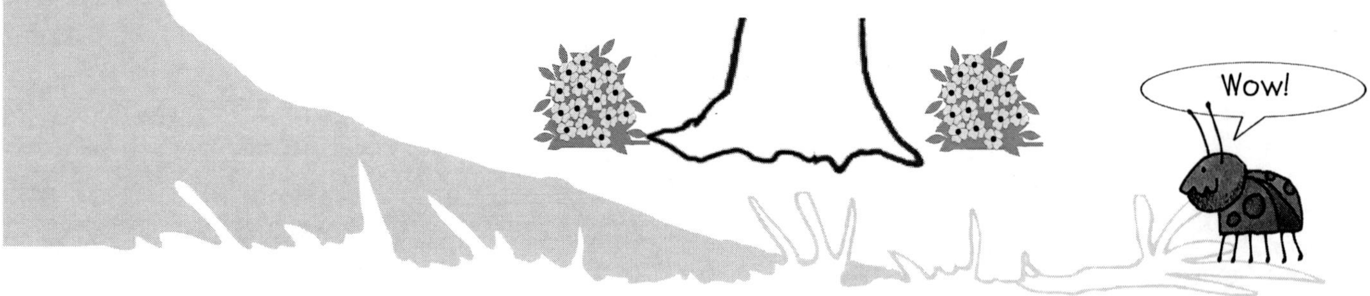

Michigan State Fish

The Michigan state fish is the brook trout. It was chosen in 1988 because it is such a popular game fish. It is the perfect fish for Michigan because it thrives in the cold water of area lakes.

Draw 6 fish in the water below. Color each one a different color.

Michigan

State Explorers

In the 1600s, explorers were sent from New France (Canada) by the governor of Quebec to find the fabled Northwest Passage. Étienne Brulé was probably the first European to visit Michigan. He explored the Upper Peninsula around 1620. In 1668, Father Jacques Marquette founded Michigan's first permanent settlement, Sault Sainte Marie.

Color the things an explorer might have used.

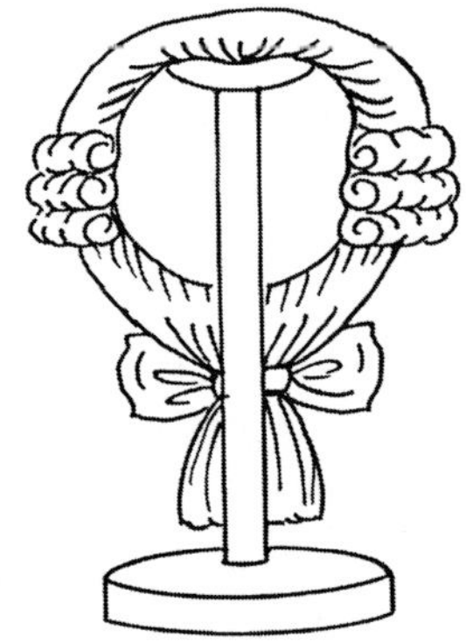

Michigan State Reptile

Michigan's state reptile, the painted turtle, was chosen in 1995 by a group of Michigan schoolchildren. The painted turtles are decorated with bright yellow and red patterns on their head, tail, limbs, and shell rims. In the winter, they sleep in the mud at the bottom of rivers, lakes, and streams. In the summer, painted turtles like to rest in the sun.

"Paint" this turtle using the color key.

COLOR KEY

R = red B = blue
Y = yellow G = green

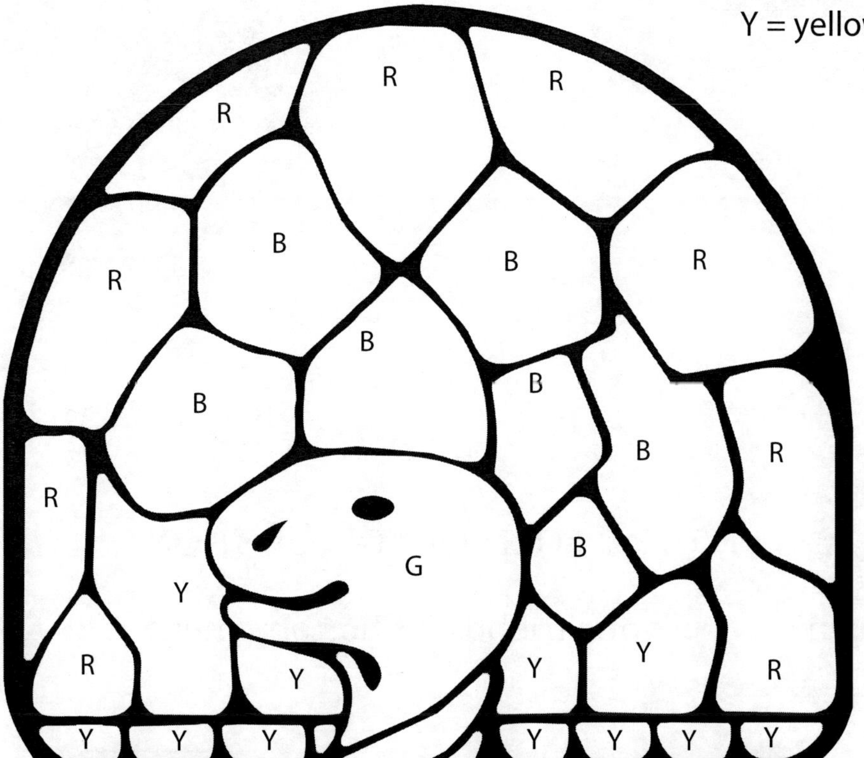

Michigan

One Day I Can Vote!

When you are 18 and register according to state laws, you can vote! So please do! Your vote counts!

Your friend is running for a class office.

She gets 41 votes!

Here is her opponent!

He gets 16 votes!

ANSWER THE FOLLOWING QUESTIONS:

1. Who won? ❑ your friend ❑ her opponent

2. How many votes were cast altogether? ☐

3. How many votes did the winner win by? ☐

Michigan State Capital

The state capital of Michigan is Lansing. It was named for John Lansing, an American Revolutionary War hero. Add your town to the map. Now add other towns you have visited.

Michigan Governor

The governor of Michigan is our state's leader.
Do some research to complete the biography of the governor.

Governor's name:

____

Paste a picture of the governor in the box.

The governor was born in this state:

____

The governor has been in office since:

____

Names of the governor's family members:

____

____

____

____

Interesting facts about the governor:

____

____

____

Michigan Crops

Some families in our state make their living from the land.

Some of our state's crops or agricultural products are:

WORD BANK

CORN	APPLES	TOMATOES
EGGS	CATTLE	MILK

UNSCRAMBLE THESE IMPORTANT STATE CROPS

RNOC ________________ KMLI ________________

PLEAPS ________________ GSEG ________________

TELACT ________________ AEMOSTTO ________________

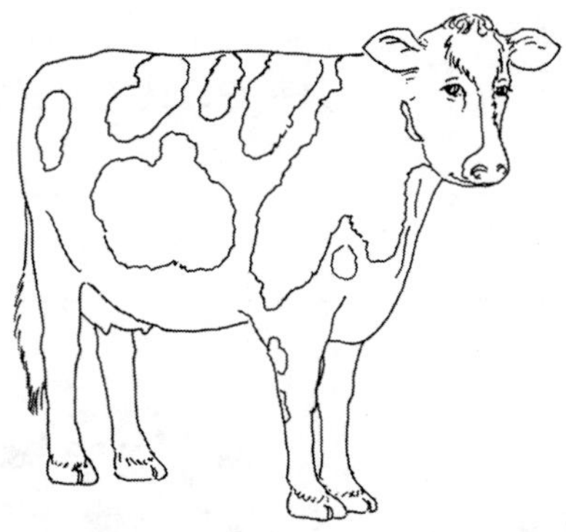

Michigan State Holidays

The people in our state enjoy celebrating holidays. Some holidays are historic. Some honor special people. Some are just for fun!

Number these holidays in order from the beginning of the year.

Columbus Day 2nd Monday in October ☐	Thanksgiving 4th Thursday in November ☐	Presidents' Day 3rd Monday in February ☐
Independence July 4 ☐	Martin Luther King, Jr. Day 3rd Monday in January ☐	New Year's Day January 1 ☐
Memorial Day last Monday in May ☐	Veterans Day November 11 ☐	Christmas December 25 ☐

Michigan
Nicknane

Our state nickname is the "Wolverine State." We are called that because people from Michigan are known for their strength and tenacity. Other nicknames that our great state has are "Great Lakes State" and "Water Wonderland."

What other nicknames would suit our state and why?

Michigan

How BIG is Our State?

Our state is the 11th largest state in the U.S. It has an area of 96,705 square miles (250,464 square kilometers).

Can you answer the following questions?

1. How many states are there in the United States?

   ____

2. This many states are smaller than our state:

   ____

3. This many states are larger than our state:

   ____

4. One mile = 5,280 ____ ____ ____ ____

   HINT: 

5. Use a map scale to determine the distance between your hometown and Washington, D.C.
   Write the distance here: ________________

ANSWERS 1.50 2.39 3.10 4.feet 5.answers will vary

Michigan People

A state is not just towns and mountains and rivers. A state is its people! But the really important people in a state are not always famous. You may know them—they may be your mom, your dad, or your teacher. The average, everyday person is the one who helps to make the state a good state. How? By working hard, by paying taxes, by voting, and by helping Michigan children grow up to be good state citizens!

Match each of these Michigan people with his/her accomplishment.

1. Ralph Bunche
2. Henry Ford
3. Clara Bartels
4. Chris VanAllsburg
5. Gerald Ford
6. Charles Lindbergh
7. Bertha Van Hoosen
8. Coleman Young

A. founded the American Medical Women's Association

B. completed the first solo transatlantic flight in 1927

C. built an automobile in 1896

D. 38th president of the United States

E. first African-American mayor of Detroit

F. Caldecott Medal-winning children's author who wrote *Jumanji*

G. Nobel Prize winner

H. the oldest immigrant to become a U.S. citizen—she was 100-years old when she was naturalized

ANSWERS: 1.G 2.C 3.H 4.F 5.D 6.B 7.A 8.E

Michigan
Gazetteer

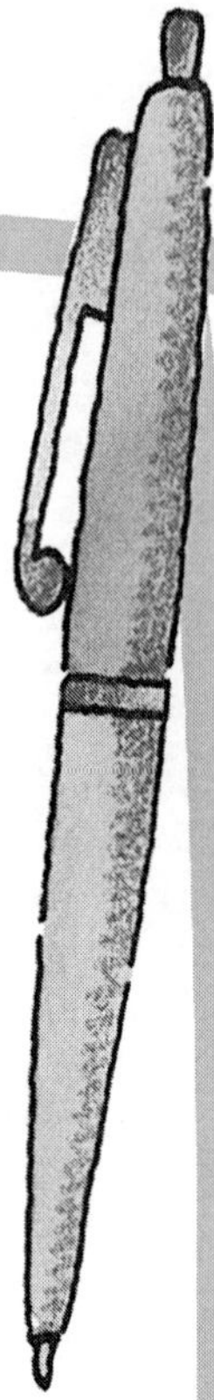

A gazetteer is a list of places. Use the word bank to complete the names of some of these famous places in our state.

1. The Grand Hotel on _ _ _ _ _ _ _ _ Island
2. The World's Largest Tire near _ _ _ _ _ _ _ _
3. The world's tallest indoor waterfall at

   _ _ _ _ _ _ _ _ _'s International Center Building
4. Walk on singing beaches at _ _ _ _ _ _ _ _ _ _
5. The _ _ _ _ _ _ _ Institute of the Arts
6. The _ _ _ _ _ _ _ Windmill of Holland
7. _ _ _ _ _ _ _, the ghost town
8. A musical fountain at _ _ _ _ _ _ _ _ _

WORD BANK

Greektown	DeZwaan
Dewey Hill	Mackinac
Fayette	Grand Haven
Dearborn	Detroit

ANSWERS: 1.Mackinac 2. Dearborn 3.Greektown 4.Grand Haven 5.Detroit 6.DeZwaan 7.Fayette 8.Dewey Hill

Michigan Neighbors

No person or state lives alone. You have neighbors where you live. Sometimes they may be right next door. Other times, they may be way down the road. But you live in the same neighborhood and are interested in what goes on there.

You have neighbors at school. The children who sit in front, beside, or behind you are your neighbors. You may share books. You might borrow a pencil. They might ask you to move so they can see the board better.

We have a lot in common with our state neighbors. Some of our land is alike. We share a common history. We care about our part of the country. We share borders. Some of our people go there; some of their people come here. Most of the time we get along with our state neighbors. Even when we argue or disagree, it is a good idea for both of us to work it out. After all, states are not like people—they can't move away!

Use the color key to color Michigan and its neighbors.

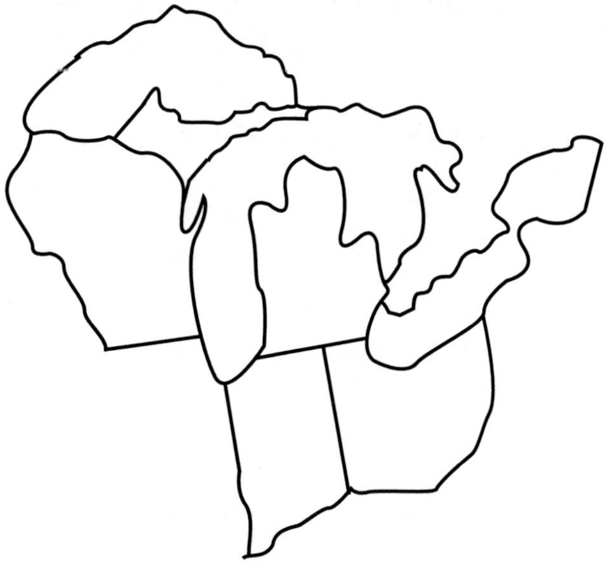

Color Key:

Michigan-yellow
Wisconsin-red
Indiana-orange
Ohio-purple
Lake Michigan, Lake Superior, Lake Huron,
Lake Erie, and Lake Ontario-blue

Michigan Highs and Lows

The highest point in our state is Mount Arvon. Mount Arvon is 1,979 feet (603 meters) above sea level.

Draw a picture of Mount Arvon.

The lowest point in our state is along Lake Erie. It is 572 feet (174 meters) above sea level.

Draw a picture of Lake Erie.

Michigan
Old Man River

Michigan has many great rivers. Rivers give us water for our crops. Rivers are also water "highways." On these water highways travel crops, manufactured goods, people, and many other things—including children in tire tubes! Here are some of Michigan's most important rivers.

GRAND	RAISIN
KALAMAZOO	SAGINAW
DETROIT	ESCANABA

MENOMINEE

Draw a kid "tubing" down a Michigan river!

Michigan Weather ... Or Not!

What kind of climate does our state have?

- Winters are usually snowy and cold
- Winter temperatures in January average around 20°F (-7°C).

- Summers are typically moist and warm
- Summer temperatures in July average around 69°F (21°C).

You might think adults talk about the weather a lot. But our state's weather is very important to us. Crops need water and sunshine. Weather can affect our state industries. Good weather can mean more for our state. Bad weather can cause problems that cost money.

ACTIVITY: Do you watch the nightly news at your house? If you do, you might see the weather report. Tonight, tune in the weather report. The reporter often talks about our state's regions, cities, towns, and neighboring states. Watching the weather report is a great way to learn about our state. It also helps you to know what to wear to school tomorrow!

What is the weather outside now? Draw a picture.

Michigan
Indian Tribes

The American Indians were first on our land, long before it was a state. Michigan's main Indian tribes include:

OJIBWA (CHIPPEWA) OTTAWA
POTAWATOMI MIAMI
HURON (WYANDOT)

Help Maize find her way through the maize (corn) field to her hut made of saplings!

Michigan
Website Page

Here is a website you can go to and learn more about Michigan:
www.state.mi.us

Design your own state website page on the computer screen below.

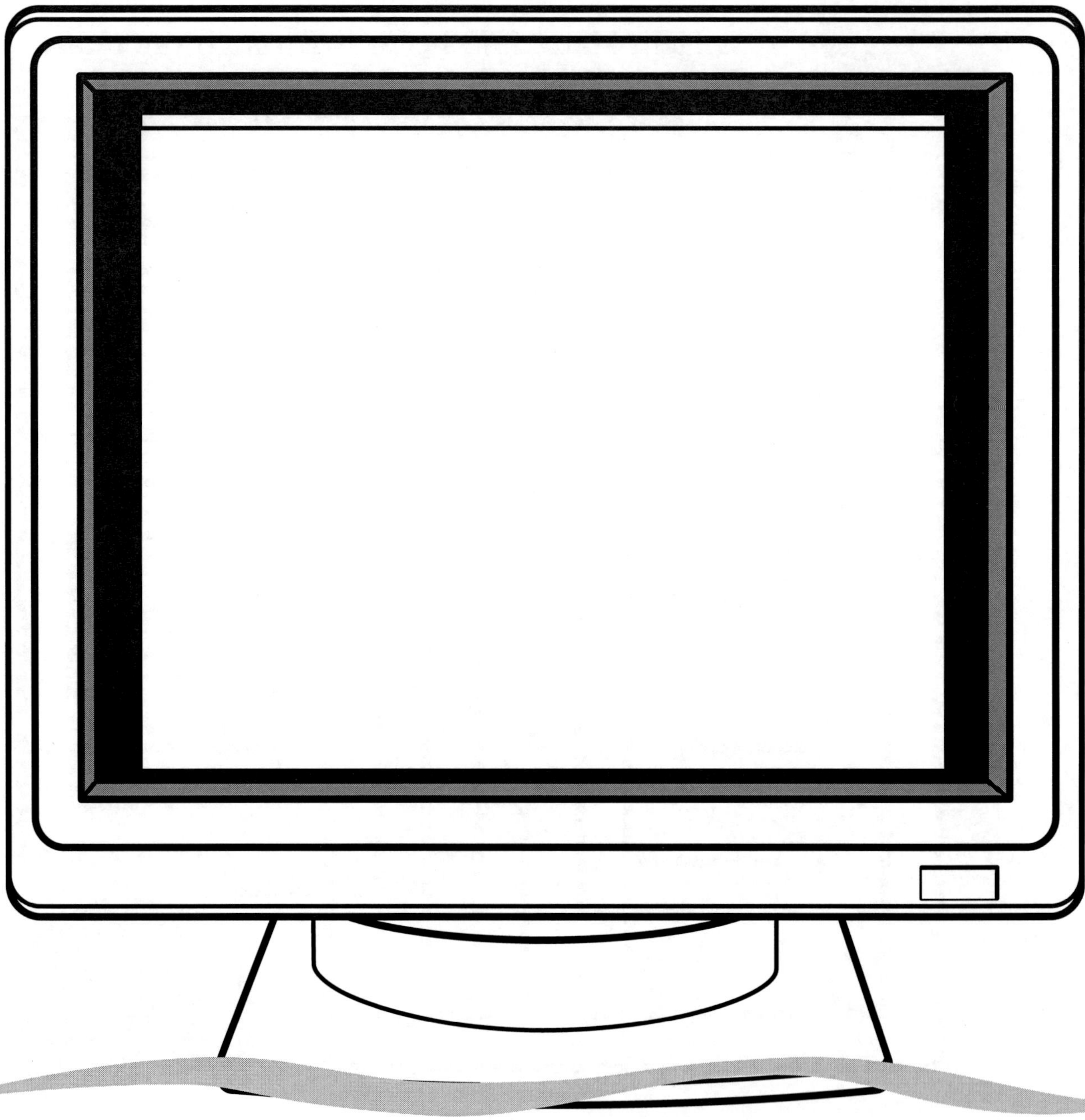

Michigan State Zoos

The Detroit Zoo in the city of Detroit was the first zoo in the country to provide open, cageless habitats for their animals.

Match the name of the zoo animal with its picture.

ZEBRA

GIRAFFE

MONKEY

BEAR

TIGER

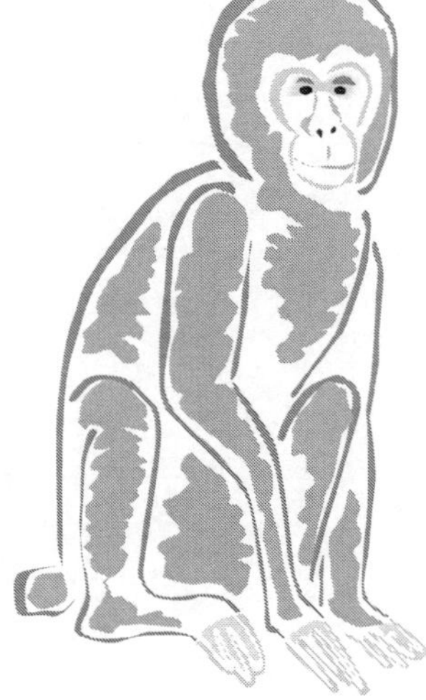

Michigan

State Song

Michigan doesn't actually have a state song, but "Michigan, My Michigan" is often used as the "unofficial" state song.

"Michigan, My Michigan"

A song to thee, fair State of mine, Michigan, my Michigan,
But a greater song than this is thine, Michigan, my Michigan,
The whisper of the forest tree, the thunder of the inland sea;
Unite in one grand symphony of Michigan, my Michigan.

I sing a State of all the best, Michigan, my Michigan;
I sing a State with riches bless'd, Michigan, my Michigan;
Thy mines unmask a hidden store, but richer thy historic lore,
More great the love thy builders bore, O Michigan, my Michigan.

1. What things unite in a grand symphony?

   ____

2. What do you think "inland sea" means?

   ____

3. What do the mines mask?

   ____

4. What is richer than what's in the mines?

   ____

5. What sounds do the trees and sea make?

   ____

ANSWERS: (may vary slightly) 1.forest trees and the inland sea 2.Lake Michigan, or Great Lakes 3.a hidden store, riches 4.history, historic lore 5.whisper and thunder

Michigan Spelling Bee!

What's All The Buzz About?

Here are some words related to your state. See if you can find them in the Word Search below.

WORD LIST

STATE	RIVER	PEOPLE	TREE	BIRD
FLAG	VOTE	FLOWER	SONG	BAY

A X N Y H N V S D G T R E P
V O T E M A C S E A B A Y E
S N B R X B R K S X B D S O
Y B P Q L S O N G R I J H P
R I V E R P P L R T Y U E L
Q R E R T Y Z E E R T O N E
R D P P A H A O N E C K A R
S X E G H B J C P W E R N I
P O B U Y U Y H E O L L D O
Q U F L A G R K R L X Z O P
Z X R D G H R E U F L L A L
M R D W Q N M N S T A T E Z

Michigan Trivia

Many people like to visit Michigan. They think it is a beautiful state and love the historic places, the beautiful scenery, and our friendly people.

Even though Michigan is called the "Wolverine State," wolverines don't actually live here!

The city of Novi was named for its earlier name of Stagecoach Stop #6, or No. VI!

Vernors ginger ale was created in Detroit by a pharmacist called away to fight in the Civil War in 1862. When he returned 4 years later, the drink he'd left in an oak case had developed a delicious gingery flavor!

Michigan is the only place in the world with a floating post office, the *J.W. Westcott II.*

Wherever you stand in Michigan, you are within 85 miles of a Great Lake.

In 1933, the first transatlantic telephone wedding took place in Detroit. A man in Detroit and a woman in Stockholm, Sweden were married over the phone!

The largest St. Bernard on record lives in Grand Rapids. Benedictine Jr. Schwarzwald Hof weighs 310 pounds (139.5 kilograms) and stands 39 inches (99 centimeters) at the shoulder!

Now write down another fact you know about Michigan here: